Mother Hen

Mother Hen

A Child of the Thirties

MEMOIR & POETRY

By Brenda Walker

THE CHOIR PRESS

First published in the United Kingdom in 2022 by
The Choir Press

ISBN 978-1-78963-324-5

Contributions by Lynette Coates & Clive Walker

Front cover photo: Brenda Mary Walker was born in July 1931 in Balham, London, the daughter of Beryl and Cyril Walters. She died in April 2020 from Covid-19 and frailty. She was our mum.

DEDICATION

Published posthumously in memory of our darling mum who died during the 2020 worldwide coronavirus pandemic, aged 88 years, on 5 April.

'Your words of wisdom, laughter and smile will always be with us for many generations to come.'

Contents

Foreword

By Lynette Coates

During my mum's lifetime she wrote many poems and stories. As a child growing up, I never realised how much she had written over the years, from about the age of 14 when she left school and went out into the world of work as a typist/shorthand secretary. In those days school exams did not exist, the Second World War was rapidly approaching, and her childhood was a hard slog.

The memoir that Mum wrote of her childhood life in the thirties, I only found after Mum sadly died during the coronavirus pandemic of 2020. Mum had written this in 2011.

While sorting out Mum's house contents upon her death, tucked away under the bed in an old, large brown envelope was Mum's life as a child, and her poetry, mostly handwritten, some typed with an old Corona typewriter. I can still remember to this day hearing Mum tapping away at a very fast rate.

Mum never had any of her poetry published. She did try but was always told that the magazine or newspaper did not have enough space left before going to print. Nowadays, with the Internet in our lives, a poem can be easily uploaded in a second.

Preface
By Lynette Coates

In this book I have included my family's memories of Mum so that the reader can try to understand her kind, caring nature and fun, fair character. Mum used to love reading her poetry to anyone who showed an interest and, in 1981, she recorded herself, with me as a child aged 11, on an old tape recorder. It was the winter, just after Christmas, snowing heavily outside and, rather than write a letter to her aunts, she suggested that we record our own musical and poetry recital. I played the recorder and harp and sung a festive hymn, and Mum narrated her poetry. Forty years later I have just found this tape recording. It brought back so many memories of that special day. We had laughed our heads off while recording it and two of the poems that Mum read out were 'The Rocking Chair' and 'I Love You Mum'. This tape recording is a priceless moment in my childhood days which I will treasure and pass onto my children ... and so the memories will continue.

Since Mum's passing, I have also taken up writing poetry. Sadly, I was unable to be with Mum when she died, due to government restrictions at the time with Covid within the UK, and I was not allowed into the hospital. Knowing that I could not hold her hand as she had done through my childhood was so difficult to accept; I could not say goodbye in person at her bedside, so I wrote a poem 'Saying Goodbye', which I have included in this book. Poetry is within us all in some way or another, it helps us see and understand the world we live in.

Introduction

By Lynette Coates

Why is this book called *Mother Hen,* I hear you ask? Mum wrote many letters of advice to me over the years on a weekly basis, especially when I left home, and she would always write her opinion and sign the letter 'Mother Hen Out'. Thankfully I kept all these letters, which have been a priceless bible of advice, little did I know that Mum kept a copy of every letter she wrote or typed just in case I ever lost one!

Mum was a stalwart for fairness in life and she would always defend and step in if she could see justice was not presenting itself in the moment. Just like a mother hen protecting her brood.

Mum's childhood memories have been published at the beginning of this book followed by family memories of Mum's life as a mum by Clive, my eldest brother, and myself. Mum led a very active, busy life and ticked off many an achievement. She grew up during the Second World War, got through the Depression and rationing, married, raised four children, emigrated to Australia and moved back to the UK, got involved in many a children's party and became the proud mum on the day of my wedding in 1997. She also became a nana to three grandchildren and saw each grandchild reach 21. Mum would get involved where she could help; raising money for many a charity, taking part in jumble sales and fetes, knitting jumpers for orphans overseas. Rambling was her favourite pastime, she loved being in the countryside. Mum also learnt to swim, a challenge for her when I was learning at school. Mum even became a Tawny Owl in Brownies!

Her motto was:

'Always live life to the full, best foot forward, keep smiling.'

All photos added by Lynette Coates and Clive Walker.

CHAPTER ONE

Childhood Memories

In Mum's words ...

I was born on 11 July 1931 at a house in Honeybrook Road, Balham, and was christened Brenda Mary Walters. Mary is a family name but where my parents got Brenda from, I do not know. I am told that around that time there was a celebrity with that name but who knows. I have been told that the Orange Men were marching around that time, or were about to, when my mum was in labour that day. I weighed 10½lbs and a telegram was sent off to my aunts telling them that 'a little apple lady' had arrived as my cheeks were so rosy (cheeks being of the facial variety!). My brother Desmond had been born about three years earlier.

Brenda in pram

Brenda aged 1

Dad worked in the pub trade all his life, but money was short in those years due to the thirties Depression, so Mum told me that she had to wait along the road for Dad to come out of the pub to give her some money to be able to buy Desmond and me some milk. She also used to spend a few pence on some roasted chestnuts from the man selling them at the kerbside.

I can vaguely remember falling down the stairs around this time ... (during my childhood years) an X-ray revealed that I had at one time broken my collarbone and I used to howl every time we went shopping in my pram; this was probably the reason why.

At some time then we moved in with Dad's mum and dad in Alexandra Gardens, Muswell Hill. Grandfather was a chimney sweep and there was a slate hanging by the door on which Granny used to write down future jobs, which were asked for by a knock on the door, as Grandad must have been able to work then. Unfortunately, he took to his bed and eventually died of sweep's cancer. I vaguely remember being taken in to see him where he lay in the downstairs front room and being held down towards his whiskered face to kiss him. It was probably not long after that he died, but I don't remember a funeral.

To recap on my address, I think it might have been Alexandra Park Gardens as we were in walking distance of the park and Desmond and I were allowed to walk there. One day we were near the boating lake in Alexandra Park and as I was walking along the low concrete edging that surrounded it, the boatman, who was watching us from his hut, yelled at me to 'Get off!' at which I promptly missed my footing and fell in. I was clutching a magic painting book, which I was still holding when I was pulled out by Desmond. Of course, the book then resembled all the colours of a rainbow much to my dismay. We were told by a passer-by to get home quickly before we caught our death, and we crossed over from the park with me crying my eyes out and Desmond in a state of shock. He was in bed afterwards affected by the trauma of it all. I don't think either of us were really told off, surprisingly, as the event happening was punishment enough.

Mum and Dad did not live together at Muswell Hill but Mum lodged with one of my friends around the corner. I was going there to play one day and spotted Mum watching us from her window. I darted back not wanting to see her thinking that she hadn't seen me but of course she had. What mother misses a trick like that! 'Why didn't you come round?' she asked me later. I had no reply to that, but she must have been quite upset at the time as I don't remember seeing her much during our stay there. I can remember, though, her taking me out to a large store where she would buy me new shoes, usually Clarks, whenever she could. Perhaps she did housework to get some cash and Dad probably gave her an allowance. Even during the war years, which were yet to come ... I had brown sensible shoes with rounded toes. The shop had a rocking horse which I used to get a ride on if we had the time; more exciting than a new pair of shoes.

Granny's house had a walled-in garden. My hands were covered in warts and, as I was told that the white sap from one of the weeds would cure them, I tried it with not a great deal of success.

Desmond slept in the same bedroom as Dad. I slept in the front bedroom with Granny as Grandad was in the downstairs front room. There was no bed for me to sleep on as Granny did not want me to share her bed with me. My bed was made up on the top of a large tin trunk, a cabin one with wooden battens around its width, which just about gave me enough room to lie down on a blanket. I don't think it could have been much thicker than that and, because the trunk was tin, it would rebound between the wooden strips so Granny would yell at me to stop moving as the sounds kept her awake. She shouted, 'Stop fidgeting,' and 'Lie still,' several times a night. It must have been as bad for her as it was for me.

There were no inside toilets then. Ours was outside the back door. Granny would use the 'po' and the room stunk of its contents. I have only realised what that smell was when, in my adult years, I have visited OAP residential homes and picked up the same 'fragrant smell'. (Apologies to any residents and/or residential homes who might read this!)

Dad used to call me 'Girlie' and we used to sit at the table while I coloured or tried early reading. Light was overhead by means of a gas mantle. These would hiss and the light was dimmed or made stronger by a metal rod with a handle that Dad pulled up or down. The mantles were very fragile and would have to be changed when they had burnt out or got broken, so we often lit a candle to save the gas and the mantles. One evening I felt my dad smacking me on my head. I didn't have long to wonder why as the smell of burnt hair was in the air. He had heard the crackle of my hair catching alight. What a good thing he was there and acted fast. I had in that minute thought he was cross with me but he was a gentle man and never once lifted his hand to us. However, there was one occasion years later, when we lived in Chelmsford, when I saw the silent but sudden loss of his temper, when he struck Desmond over something I thought trivial at the time – but it was enough for him to get into a sudden rage.

Dad had two sisters, Mildred and Muriel, who were tyrants to us two kids, well, they were to me anyway, and were always correcting us especially on our manners at the table. They were obviously intent on helping Dad and Granny bring us up and were probably very helpful kind-hearted women, but I hated them. I once sat on their toilet wondering where the paper was (squares of newspaper sometimes). I couldn't decide what the cloth hanging by the loop on the door was for, never having had one on a door before ... so I used it! That action resulted definitely in being SENT TO BED.

One of the sisters had a daughter called Elizabeth, really spoilt, who had a tutor in to educate her. I expect the rule of having to eat everything on your plate came from the two of them. If we didn't eat or left anything from any meal on our plate it was put in front of us at the next mealtime, and the next. So, there were plenty of occasions when eating the cold food, something I really hated, would make me retch, but eventually after the next couple of mealtimes, you either ate it or got rid of it somehow.

Desmond used to make some pocket money following the coalman's horse and cart picking up the manure as it went by the house. He either got a few pence for it or it went into the garden. He also collected old bikes to take apart and make up to be rideable, up and down outside as the road was hilly. I was given pocket money to spend, not much, but a penny went a long way on, yes, you've guessed it, sweets. Four Golly Bars were 1d, or two sweets and two Golly Bars, maybe a sherbet dab or sweet cigarettes. I liked to get the ones that lasted longest ... decisions, decisions.

Boat Race Day was an exciting event, although I was never taken to watch it, and we used to wait to hear the result. 'What team do you support, Oxford or Cambridge?' I was asked. I chose Oxford as I preferred dark blue to light blue. Over the years, I've still watched the race, on TV now of course, as it has always been a tradition to keep up by me.

During the time when my Grandad was dying, or very ill anyway, two of my mum's sisters. Gwen and Floss (or should I write Gwendoline and Florence) came to see us. Little Granny as we used to call her (Big Granny being my mum's mum) had obviously been doing her best to look after Desmond and me but was stressed because of Grandad, and they could see I was being neglected. They were appalled to see that my auburn curly hair was full of nits and that I seemed to have been constantly wearing red wellies that were a size too small. When they approached Granny and asked her whether it would help if they took me away for a while, she would have been relieved I expect. I can remember being dumped in the bath as soon as we got to their house, boots and all. I had been wearing them without socks and they were stuck to my feet with the perspiration. Because they had been too small for me, I have always had three toes on both feet that are very misshapen.

I can't remember going back to Granny but I obviously did as I started school, which was situated at the bottom of the road; a few years ago there was still a school on that site. All I can remember of the start of my education is marching in to the sound of a band recording and picking up a rush mat, which we were to sit on in the hall. This had to be done very quietly without anyone speaking. I don't remember taking part in any lessons or any of the teachers.

The only incident I can recall is a man coming in to remind us of road safety and asking us if anyone knew the Crossing Song. The firm that manufactured Ovaltine had created a tune which had the words, 'We are the Ovaltineys, happy boys and girls'* and, after a couple more lines which I don't remember, ended with 'Look to the left, and look to the right and we will never get run over.' Well, I knew it and was the first person to put up my hand and volunteer to go up on stage and sing it! After my performance I got the prize of a small Scottie dog with a squeak in its tummy which I decided to press at various times afterwards, much to the headmistress's annoyance who told me not to do so.

---

* These are the words as Mum remembered them. The original song began 'We are the Ovaltineys, little girls and boys'.

CHAPTER TWO

I can't remember that I went out with both Mum and Dad at any time either before or after their separation, between 1931 and 1945, when I was born and they were divorced. Perhaps we did but I have no memory of it.

Before we went to live in Muswell Hill one of my earliest memories would be when we lived in a bungalow at Woodley just outside Reading, not far from the airport, wherever that was then and probably still is for small aircraft. I can remember waiting for the milkman who delivered by horse and cart but I don't think I was allowed to carry in the milk which had been poured into a jug.

Age 2 wearing the teddy bear coat

Age 4 in Woodley

Auntie Gwen visited us after she had been on the maiden voyage of the *Queen Mary* to America. She brought me back a dress and a coat, the coat being made of fur-like material resembling a teddy bear which I called just that, 'My teddy bear coat'. It had very large mother-of-pearl buttons. I wore and wore it until it had got too small for me when Mum told me that I was unable to make use of it any longer. The buttons were kept in her button box for years and I had them when she died. I still wish that I had them but in a moment of generosity I gave them to a friend for her to sew on to her pearly queen outfit. A photograph shows me standing on the mound of grass in our Woodley garden wearing the dress with my mop of curls outlining my face. I was auburn in those early years!

Dad was given the chance to start and run an accumulator business, Auntie Gwen's friend had given him some money, but it wasn't a success. He had to visit customers and pick the accumulators up for recharge but he never seemed to get up in time to do so. If he was still working as a bar cellar man until late at night, I don't suppose he could rouse himself in the mornings to do so.

Dad and Mum got back together again and we moved down to Walton-on-the-Naze, Essex. Dad's brother Frank was a fisherman at Frinton-on-Sea. Dad got a job at the Albion right on the front. It was probably about 1937–38 because although I can remember attending a school, I have no other memories. We lived in two houses there, one in a road right next to the post office and the second not far from the school. During this time, Mum had furniture and bedding on hire purchase, and anything that wasn't hire purchase was second-hand.

There was a cabinet wind-up gramophone with a few 78 rpm black records. We had no other music available but one of them must have been a favourite of mine as I can only remember 'It's my Mother's Birthday Today' droning along as it slowly ran down and, then, me frantically winding the handle so that it used to go so fast that it sounded like a jumbled parrot. Then, when the needles got too blunt, we would have to wait until Mum got some more. If there was a scratch on the record it would keep repeating and you would have to lift the needle arm and hopefully place it back on to the record without it slurring and causing more damage.

When Mum ran out of money to pay the weekly instalments for the hire purchase, the inevitable happened and a man came to take away the furniture. It broke my heart to see it all go and, as I think back, I can see how upset she was. That day I had come home from school or from the seafront and found that I had a tea chest to sit on. They became quite regular features in my life over the forthcoming years.

I used to love going down to the sea carrying a bucket and spade and just wearing my costume. It was only a few minutes' walk from Dad's pub where he worked. Could you imagine allowing the kids to do that now? Dad would have known all the men around; they were probably clientele at the pub. One fellow was called Tony who was also a fisherman and we used his boat called the *Y-NOT*. He used to allow me to sit right up at the front for free and, if any kids seemed too nervous to go for a ride, he would shout out that they should be like the little girl in front who looked as though she was enjoying the waves – and then they seemed to get the courage to get in. I was never sick as we bobbed along! One day I had some added excitement when I noticed some driftwood coming in on the tide but the sea was too deep for me to attempt to get it. Someone pulled it out for me and I lugged it home like a prized possession and gave it to my mum at the back door. It would be used for fuel.

On the beach, I made friends with a boy called Barrie Le Boutillier, over from the Channel Islands with his parents. When the war broke out in 1939, they were uncertain at first whether to return because of the threat of invasion. They chose to return while they could still get across the Channel. Unfortunately, they would have encountered plenty of Germans eventually when they occupied the Islands. We never heard from them again. As children we never realised the seriousness of it all, it was just something happening in our young lives that seemed exciting. We all listened to Winston Churchill's speech and afterwards I ran along the beach shouting 'The Germans

Brenda on the beach with brother Desmond

are coming, the Germans are coming,' and was told off by bystanders for doing so.

One of my favourite places was a library where for 1d you could get a book. It wasn't a proper library but books were kept on shelves at the back of a newsagent's / sweet shop. I was an avid reader (being hopeless at sums) and *Doctor Dolittle* and *Swallows and Amazons* are still read today – and of course Enid Blyton. I could get lost in those stories and Mum was always telling me to get my head out of a book because that's all I did it seemed. As I got older, I used to write reams of my own stories in lined exercise books which were promptly discarded – or lost on purpose by Mum I expect. I also copied pictures in pen and ink, one was of two Scottie dogs seated on a chair which I was very pleased with, and I kept it for a number of years.

The invasion became threatening to anyone on the east coast and Dad got a job at The Spotted Dog in Chelmsford. Our new accommodation was a three-bedroomed, plus kitchen, flat in Tindal Street. The pub was opposite, so Dad didn't have far to go to work. The flat was over a butcher's shop. There was a very small kitchen with a window overlooking another belonging to the photographer's opposite where you could see him at his kitchen window. I doubt he had a special place for developing the films. Mum reckoned that if we could see him then he could see us, and she would pull the curtain across, especially if we had a light on whilst we washed. We only had a bowl in the sink for this purpose (plus washing-up as well!) and had no bath for the five or six years we lived there.

There were three other rooms and you stepped down into each. The first was our living room with cupboards each side of the fireplace. The next room was Dad and Mum's bedroom and the next one along the passageway, Desmond and I shared. There were two windows in this and one in each of the others. After these rooms the passage led to a dead end and was blocked by a partition wall. The rest of our furniture and belongings were stored here.

Beyond the partition were storerooms belonging to International Stores and sometimes we could hear raised voices from the staff. Running along the front was a balcony, about 2 feet wide and the depth of a large kitchen swing bin. Mum planted up large flowerpots (no Gro-bags then) with tomato plants and, whatever she did to them, she certainly got us a good supply of vitamin C.

Mum was always a very plump person and the fried bread and bread and dripping she gave us to 'fill a corner' didn't help her. She used to have great difficulty climbing out the window of the sitting room, using the couch as her first step, but she managed it in order to water and pick the tomatoes. There was no thought of health and safety in those days. Once out there, any passer-by, customers going to the pub, Yanks and our soldiers with their girls would call out to her, 'Come on then, Mum, show us your legs.'

My world was what I saw outside on the street from the windows. Mum and I used to lean over the sill so that we could see what was happening outside, which character was going by, and then duck down whenever we needed, which was quite often as our elbows used to ache so, or we were laughing so much together and nearly crying with laughter as well. Mum could always have a good old laugh with me, but at other times she could be feeling so miserable and depressed through the anxieties of the war and her home and married life, plus the fact that my family – then and now – are all autistic to a certain degree; my habit/tic then was that I used to sniff, sniff and more sniffs.

Obviously, life then wasn't safe, secure and was very uncertain, which didn't help me and hundreds of other kids who had it far worse. I must have driven Mum mad and she would shout at me to 'Shut up' and 'Stop sniffing' and wallop me across the side of my head with an intensity that used to send me across the room, usually into the kitchen cupboards. I hated this and I used to go to school not acknowledging that I had a mum at all, and at night I used to think to myself, oh she hasn't hit me today. I never told her if there was any activity on at school, e.g. sports day, which I was hopeless at anyway, and she sometimes asked me a week later why I hadn't told her about it. What could I say in answer to her? If I can remember how I felt, I must have felt very guilty.

It was suggested that Desmond could be evacuated by ship to Canada. I was too young but Mum decided that we were to stay together. A good decision because that ship was torpedoed, and all life was lost. Mum would try and wake Desmond and I once the sirens had started so that we could walk to one of the underground shelters at the Corn Exchange. It was horrid, dark and cold, and very smelly, and we were expected to stay there until the all-clear. It was impossible to sleep, and with all the efforts of trying to get us two up, with a bomb dropping nearby, and the blast making the slatted wooden blinds (fixed to the sides of the window frames with wing nuts) shake, the air raid warden would often be shouting, 'Put that light out!' By the time that had happened a few times, Mum decided we wouldn't go down the shelter but that, if we were going to die, we would go together in the comfort of our beds and Desmond and I got used to all the racket and slept through it usually.

The most frightening noise was the doodlebugs flying over, droning away. If the noise was overhead and then stopped you knew you were safe as it would glide away from our home. If it stopped a distance away it could be gliding towards us and we were the target it might hit. A lot of areas didn't make it but we were some of the lucky ones, perhaps someone was looking after us, we thought. We used to reckon that we had a better chance to stay put as the floor/shop ceiling was reinforced by steel rods fitted for the butchers to hang and pull around the sides of meat.

The butcher's shop in Tindal Street in the 1920s. Brenda lived in the flat above the shop. Photo obtained from Essex Record Office, Essex County Council (Document Reference D/F 269/1/448).

CHAPTER THREE

Dad had to go into the Home Guard (Dad's Army) as his age was beyond call-up papers. He had to be fitted with a uniform, but the one that was provided was OK for the tunic but the trousers were miles too long although they did fit around his waist. Mum had to turn his trousers up, no sewing machine in those days. Dad was a short and stocky build, and he drank and smoked so that didn't help his weight and health; as well as the passive smoking involved through working behind a bar. Years later he was found to have an affected heart valve, which he would have had for most of his life without an earlier diagnosis, so the smoke and drink wouldn't have helped over the years. He died at the age of 64. Mum also died at this age due to breast cancer, but some years later in this story. I am not really surprised with all the stress that she had gone through.

If women were old enough, they were called up for service into one of the forces. Desmond might have been exempt through working at Crompton Parkinson's as a draughtsman; this was accepted as important work. Being an older mother with children, Mum was expected to volunteer for voluntary work. Mum was a bit dismayed at this at first but found that being amongst a lot of other women gave her some freedom of speech and movement. When I used to go and meet her after I got back home from school, she would come out with the rest of the workers laughing away.

I used to come home from school on the bus from Princes Road School, which had an infants and juniors section – plus another building which housed the rest of us kids who would be leaving at 14 years of age. They raised the school leaving age to 15 the year after I had left but I missed that, much to my delight. There is still a school on that site and I often wonder, should I send them an email and ask if they would like to have their Domestic Science book back? But I still use the hints and recipes in it now.

I wasn't a very bright scholar, I shouldn't have really gone in for the 11-plus and had already been told by my teacher that I hadn't got a hope in passing, but Mum thought I was worthy of at least having a go. It was held in the County Hall: I think the morning subject was Maths and I gave up trying to do that halfway through; I never could understand the decimal point let alone anything else. After lunch I was in an absolute panic as I couldn't remember where the classroom was let alone take an exam in English. The corridors seemed endless but luckily someone must have seen my distress and showed me the way and I just made it. I never passed, of course, which came as no surprise.

At school, I enjoyed English, Spelling, and Geography as it involved drawing maps, but being left-handed and looking at the British Isles, it took me a while to remember which was east and west! History I hated, dates had to be remembered and who cared during the war years when the Battle of Waterloo was or the date of Magna Carta (when were those anyway?).

After enduring chronic stomach ache for, it seemed, years (Dad would bring me over some peppermint cordial), it turned out that I needed an appendix operation. During this operation, I was found to have a gland that could develop into tuberculosis. The combination of being allowed extra milk but not allowed to do exercise in school resulted in me being a little on the plump side.

Our headmistress was called Miss Howard and the other teachers were Miss Manse, Miss Alden and our Domestic Science teacher was appropriately called Mrs Cook; teachers took several subjects. Domestic Science involved bringing ingredients from home to be able to make up the recipes that the teacher had decided we should learn. Mum, as usual, hadn't got enough cash to buy all those bits and pieces or, if in fact, they had to be taken out of the family's rations. All I ever made was blancmange out of cornflour, colouring and flavouring, milk, and a bit of sugar. The bowls used to stand on the ground outside the classroom with a saucer on them otherwise you would have to carry them home with dust on the skin, YUK! The teacher gave up asking me where my ingredients were eventually. If you were lucky, you might be chosen to be one of two girls to go and tidy up the storeroom, an enviable task as it gave you the chance ... if you were very careful, to pinch a few currants from the fruit jars; better also if there had been a few dropped on to the floor.

I didn't have many special friends but was not necessarily excluded from conversations with others. Joan Smith, Betty Nicholls, Yvonne Clements are some of the names I can remember. Some girls were obviously more mature than a lot of us but I can't remember any unwanted pregnancies though it wouldn't have been discussed or been apparent to us.

Dad once came to meet me at the school gate and we caught the bus home; I can remember being very surprised to see him. Otherwise, the only door to our flat was left unlocked and I would go in, up the stairs, and find Dad snoring his head off, lying on the settee by the lounge window having come in from his job at the pub opposite when it had closed at 2 p.m. Mum would leave a dinner on a plate for me, to be heated up over a saucepan of water, which should have been put on by Dad. But this task allotted to him was never, or hardly ever, carried out. So, if Mum found out when she came in from work that I had had to wait before I could eat my meal, she would tell him off. It was better to say the deed had been done. I did have school dinners at first but they were terrible. Stringy meat, overdone cabbage, watery gravy, and weevil in the semolina, tapioca, YUK! Hard-baked squares of what was supposed to be pastry and a scraping of jam and cream, which was the 'shaving cream' variety. Rice pudding was nice, though, but it wouldn't have gone down very well if today's children had to eat it. You were allowed to take your own sandwiches, which I did in the end. Bread was rationed and was neither brown nor white but a grey dingy colour as other ingredients had been added to give it bulk. I used to take an Oxo cube as a drink and once I was made by a teacher to add milk to it as she said there was no goodness in it made with water; I hated that and was promptly sick.

Whenever the sirens sounded, we had to file into various air raid shelters allocated to each class. This didn't help our concentration or schooling as the light was very dim and lessons were not really continued properly while we were in there. However, as I had been told on several occasions that I wasn't a very good scholar, I had come to the conclusion that you either worry or you put the fact aside as I seemed to do; so I just concentrated on the subjects I liked.

Looking back on my childhood now, I just hated most of school and was so pleased when I could leave at 14 years of age before they made 15 years the leaving age the following year.

CHAPTER FOUR

My half-brother Ivan was born in 1945 and this resulted in my parents splitting up and their consequent divorce. Mum, Ivan and I stayed in the flat but Dad was offered accommodation in the pub where he worked across the road from us, The Spotted Dog. The day he left I became very upset sitting on my bed crying that I wanted to stay with Mum (which after he had gone Mum picked me up on). I had got muddled up with the legal wording that he was to provide me with maintenance of £2 per week which I then had to pick up from a solicitor, which made me feel very uncomfortable. This was to be paid until I was 16 years old.

Dad was allowed access once a week and we would visit the Regent Theatre or one of the three cinemas, usually the more modern one of them called The Ritz. The Pavilion and The Select usually catered for the younger kids and these establishments were re-titled The Fleapit and The Bughouse respectively, but whether they 'lived' up to their names, luckily, I never found out. I always enjoyed these outings except for the time we went to see *Dr Jekyll and Mr Hyde* when I had nightmares for weeks afterwards. Mum would be watching for us walking back with our arms linked behind our backs and when I got in, she would comment on what we looked like … lovers she said, but of course she was jealous of the attention given by him to me, which she reckoned she had never had in their married life.

I can remember the King speaking to us over the airwaves (the wireless not radio then), and we used to try and will him to get the words out, but eventually he did so much better. Then, sometimes it was 'Germany calling, Germany calling' and Lord Haw-Haw going on and on expecting us to listen to the lies; I expect our transmitters were doing the same back. We all seemed to feel very patriotic towards England then and Churchill's rousing speech 'We shall fight on the beaches . . . ', helped us all to put up with our lot.

Whenever there was a rumour that some food or essential item, soap, etc. was going to come in, Mum would send me out with the ration books to see what I could get, sometimes not knowing what the item was. This was usually before school so if the queue didn't move quickly enough, I would be late getting there or often not get there at all. It might be nothing to get very excited over, an ounce of butter, margarine, or cheese, one egg or some broken biscuits. You would hand over the money, which was placed in a screwed container that was twisted like a light bulb into a cable line above our heads. A handle on a cord, like the sort on an overhead toilet cistern, would be tugged and off went the container to the cashier; if any change was required it would then be sent back again.

It didn't take much for me to enjoy a day off school but I wasn't skiving when I was getting acute stomach aches, which was eventually diagnosed to be appendicitis, but the school officer still came around to see why I was away.

I can never remember going out with my mum and dad on any outings, or my brother Desmond for that matter. Every day I would push Ivan around the park and all the streets of the town. Mum did take us to London, by steam train then, to see the outside of Buckingham Palace and to Madame Tussauds; this was after the war had ended. She told us that when she visited there years before one of the waxworks was of a policeman. He frightened her to death whilst she was going past him when he patted her on the shoulder and asked her how she was! It didn't happen when we went though.

We would also get on the bus and go to the woods at Billericay in Essex to pick bluebells, which was allowed then, but it was a shame they had wilted before we got home.

I knew several other girls that were Brownies and Guides and this interested me enough to ask Mum if I could join but I received the answer 'No'. That was because she couldn't afford the uniform – so that was that and was the end of that idea. Even if they might have offered her the chance of a second-hand uniform, I doubt that she would have accepted it as it would have been charity in her eyes. Nowadays 'charity' shops are doing very well; how times change.

I fancied joining in to get out into the countryside with Uncle Arthur and do some tracking, which Murray (my cousin), Desmond and I did when we spent our summer holidays with them at Bramley. We used to have a head start on Uncle Arthur and we scurried on ahead so that he was miles behind, or so we thought, and then hide in the bracken and not turn up at the house until teatime.

I loved the school subject of Nature. Another girl and I had chosen to illustrate a flower, me to draw it and she to write down the description. I made a good job dissecting the head of it but goodness knows how I managed as, like idiots, we had chosen a wildflower Shepherd's purse which is one of the smallest. I had already collected it and mounted with others in a scrapbook. That's not encouraged now of course.

I used to read all the articles published in the *Evening News* by Frances Pitt and cut them out to read again.

The nearest I ever got to religion was when Mrs Cheyney, the landlady of The Spotted Dog asked Mum if I would like to go with her to the cathedral as she went there on Sundays to the service and communion. I used to enjoy the hymns, the stained-glass windows and the peace of the surroundings, but I thought that the clergyman's sermon was very boring and used to try not to yawn and fidget. Instead, I found that when he stood up in the pulpit the sun shone directly on to his glasses and the reflections in them made his eyes look like golden orbs, making him look like an evil demon rather than a member of the clergy. Mrs Cheyney suggested to Mum that I could go with her to start the process of becoming confirmed but Mum told her that could be decided when I was older; when I could make up my own mind which church I wanted to belong to (but I never have) – although I still love singing the hymns.

Mum made sure that I went to a Sunday school and I attended the Baptist church for that. We collected texts and puts them in our bibles in the appropriate places, along with the four-leaf clovers that I had found. The teacher was a spinster who was obviously hoping to get us interested in her readings; we were probably quite horrid to her when we lost interest in it and decided it wasn't for us and left, either much to her dismay or delight.

CHAPTER FIVE

Our radio went wrong and we took it along to be repaired because we were lost without it. It had been away about two weeks, as they had to find parts for it, and then the shop was bombed. Because of this (their surviving records showed our radio had gone up as well) they offered to replace it in the bomb damage assessment, and we were left with a much better radio than we had started with.

Mum used to go down once a week when vans used to draw up and park on ground behind the Corn Exchange. These were filled with possessions from houses in the Blitz and re-sold (the start of car boot sales, perhaps?). Mum would be in there from the start before the men had even unwrapped the packages. Once she found a fruit bowl, as she called it, which should have had a lid, and it had previously been a vegetable dish in a dinner service. It had a silver edge all around the top which attracted her to it and we did in fact use it as a fruit bowl afterwards. If I had all the Royal Doulton pieces now that she had bought, they would have been worth something for *Cash in the Attic*. I still have two pieces but they have got damaged during my numerous moves.

We used to take Ivan in his pushchair and be outside the Shire Hall every Sunday where the Salvation Army played. When it had finished it was time for the band to start marching down Chelmsford High Street and we would leave and walk ahead very quickly to be able to turn to be able to let him see them marching towards us. He would shake his feet and hands in excitement as they passed and then we would run down the passageways behind the shops and come out further down so that he could see them a second time. By this time the first march was finishing.

I was often left to look after Ivan when Mum went out of an

evening (of course, nowadays that wouldn't be allowed as I think I was still only about 13 years old). Sometimes she used to stay over until the early milk train or come back late evening, but mostly I would stay awake listening for her footsteps coming down the road and was so relieved when she had come up the stairs. I guess my stressed life started then without realising, though, I didn't realise why I was anxious at the time.

This was after the war had finished, in 1946. Ivan needed feeding and changing which I worried about; I was too young for that responsibility I guess, and I would keep thinking what I had to do if Mum didn't get home until breakfast when I was solely in charge of the baby. It is no wonder that I developed shingles and was sent to stay awhile with Auntie Maudie, Uncle Mungo and Murray. They lived in Bramley, near Guildford, Surrey, and I attended the primary school there (where it still stands today). The hall was separated by a wooden partition, one class on each side and a coke boiler. Sometimes, for group activities, the partition was folded back. We both went there for summer holidays and enjoyed the freedom of the fields opposite, now it's all a built-up area. Whenever we heard a train coming, we would race out of the house and across to the metal fencing to see if we could get there in time. Innocent pleasures.

I went to Bristol with them when Uncle Mungo was transferred there with the BBC London. Christmases as well. They paid for me to go to Clark's College for some education where they made me write with my right hand only, as left handers were made to do often. I can still write with both hands but with a completely different writing style for each. If I ever had a handwriting expert give an analysis of it, I wonder what they would make of each style.

Uncle Mungo was transferred again, this time to Wales. Murray told me that there would be ponies for us to ride on and I got excited not realising that I wasn't to be included in the plan. Mum had told Auntie Maudie that she wanted me home again. It was sometimes said that, as a baby during the thirties Depression, Auntie Maudie had wanted to take me over and possibly adopt me but Mum hadn't agreed to that. I was taken back home to see Mum and I presume then that I knew that I was there to stay. When I got up the next day I remember asking 'Where was Auntie Maudie?' Mum replied something to the effect that she had had to leave early before I was awake. I was more upset that she hadn't said goodbye to me, (she hadn't been able to do so for fear of getting upset herself) and I couldn't get over the fact that she had left me without doing so. You can never forget these incidents . . . ever!

Tindal Street Butchers worked out to be quite a good source of food for us. Not necessarily handouts of the meat rations when supplies came in but other sources of nutrients. Marrow bones were practically thrown down the saw-dusted stairs to their basement and were always available to Mum for her home-made soup which we practically lived on. I still have the plates/bowls that we ate it from. She used to boil the marrow bones up, twice, so two saucepans of stock, let it cool overnight, scrape off the fat, extract the thick jelly and then sometimes even start the process again until the jelly got to be liquid with obviously hardly any nutrients in it by then. In went the vegetables or anything else available, including a tin of baked beans. It was delicious.

Perhaps my good health now, at nearly 80, is due to Mum's soups that we all used to tuck into. Who knows? Fried bread didn't seem to do us any harm and there was always a jar of Marmite to dip into to smear on the top. And we ate rice puddings and semolina (without the weevil). Offal wasn't a popular buy and, because of that, it wasn't rationed so we got used to that very quickly. No one could be a fussy eater then and you were just glad to sit down to have something tasty – whatever the ingredients were. Bread was a dull grey and I didn't have far to queue up as there was a shop at the end of the road.

CHAPTER SIX

I gave up arranging to meet friends as they sometimes never turned up before we went into the cinema – so I would go in alone. Front rows 1/0d, and back rows 1/9d (one shilling and ninepence, so nearly 20p now). I just loved all the films (apart from *Dr Jekyll and Mr Hyde*). A lot of old ones were repeated often. They still are now and sometimes even the ones that I saw as a child! There were still new ones being made later. Clark Gable in *Gone with the Wind*, *Scott of the Antarctic*, and Ronald Colman in *Lost Horizon*. I used to get so excited sitting there on my own, not having a friend next to me to talk to about it with, so I used to cross my arms and hug my sides tight. Would one call this a pleasure? Films and books used to take me away from reality.

As I got older my maturity became apparent, and every time I went to the cinema, I hoped that a pervert would not be sitting next to me (though I wouldn't have known that word then). A knee touching mine so subtly that on the first occasion, I thought it was just a shift in the seating of whoever was next to me, but he had moved along to be nearer to me without me realising. The next time, and it seemed several times afterwards and on other occasions, when I had kept moving along the row of seats, I had the courage to stamp down on his feet and made it obvious to those around me that he should leave me alone. Nothing was said to him though.

I was a few rows in front of my brother once whilst watching *Scott of the Antarctic* when the usherette produced an ice cream for me saying it was from the young man behind, I turned around and there was Desmond ... with a girlfriend ... showing his affection and generosity towards his sister, to make an impression on the girlfriend, I guess. About the first and last time that happened,

Brenda: aged 18 or 19

maybe he ran out of girls to impress, or we were not in the cinema again together.

My teenage years started and Mum had noticed a group of girls going into the alley behind the pub. This led to a door with stairs up to quite a smallish room where a lady called Miss Elsie Hull taught shorthand and typing. Mum came back and we decided that I should also go along to learn. Unless you were very clever and passed matriculation exams (O levels) there were not a lot of jobs on offer, only domestic, shop or factory worker, or office work if you were lucky. On the first evening of study, I came home very excited showing Mum the Pitman's shorthand, 'squiggles' as I called them, and repeating 'pee, bee, tee, dee, chay, jay, a. e. i. o. u' with hard and soft pronunciations. Miss Hull would time us and we would take speed tests on both the typewriter and in shorthand.

It was 1944 and my childhood had now gone by. I was nearly 14 years of age and I started work at a solicitors office only a short walk away from home. I was the office junior, answering the phone. This was an upright black one with an earpiece hung on the side, like you would see in a museum today, a general runabout. Another duty was going to the café next door, also a bread shop, to pick up a trayful of coffee pots and teapots and the cups and saucers. Why they didn't make their own I do not know. I could hardly manage to carry that lot up the stairs to the offices above.

Eventually, after a move into new premises in the London Road, the firm amalgamated, and I became a shorthand typist. Touch typing didn't come into it, even when typing envelopes as a junior, as speed was essential, so I had adapted to type quickly but got into a routine with the alphabet.

Conveyances had to be typed on parchment and as this was to be a legal document you were not allowed to make a mistake otherwise you would be deducted 10 shillings (50p) from your wages. I only started on 7/6d per week (75p) so that would have been a catastrophe. The more you tried not to make a mistake the more you seemed to make one, but we were crafty and if you were lucky enough not to be seen you could just about delete the mistake with the edge of a razor and then rubbing your thumbnail over the roughened edge would smooth the paper down. Typing over it again, it wasn't noticeable unless under close scrutiny. Of course, if you typed a couple of letters wrong and had to scrap the whole lot it was no use throwing it into the wastepaper basket as they would be checked at the end of the day. I made sure my bag for work was large enough to take the evidence home, with a sigh of relief, and my wages intact.

I did change jobs several times. My second was after I had come back from a few days' holiday only to be told by the chief secretary that I was no longer needed. This was because I had neglected to type up the accounts, which were of course very important as there would be no payments by clients otherwise. I was asked to stand before him in his office and had to account why I hadn't done them. I told him I was unable to decipher them as he had gone so fast it was beyond my ability to keep up with him. Why hadn't I told him, he asked. Well, I should have done, shouldn't I? I was 14 years of age after all. In those days the 'boss' especially a solicitor, like a doctor, was held in a sort of reverence and awe. He told me that I had a week's notice *in lieu*. I had to ask what that meant never having heard it before. When I was told I could leave with a week's wages straight away, I DID.

Another reason for my dismissal might have been the fact that if someone wanted a typewriter you were expected to carry it down the stairs. This one had a longer carriage and as I struggled to carry it down the carriage swung along, hit the banister, and I dropped it with an almighty crash. Horror of horrors, what a noise, and they all came out to see what damage had been done to the typewriter!

My childhood had ended. Now, what other delights in life awaited me?

Brenda at work with typewriter

Brenda Walker.

_____

31ˢᵀ May 2011.

_____

Nana to Samuel, Grace & Calum
Love you all —
Nana xXx

Following on from Mum's childhood memoirs, the next chapters
describe how she met Dad, and their family life in the
1970s and 1980s.

CHAPTER SEVEN

When Mum Met Dad

By Lynette Coates

Mum met my dad, Reginald Victor Walker – Reg for short – in the mid-1950s at the main post office in Dorking, Surrey. I remember Mum telling me that they passed each other in the queue for many weeks, Dad paying in the wages for a company he worked for nearby and Mum probably sending a letter off to one of 'the aunts'! Mum and Dad courted mainly at Worthing seafront; I have many a photo of them sitting in the old-fashioned deckchairs along the pier laughing their heads off with Dad always holding a pipe or smoking one with his hair slicked back with oil, the fashion statement in those days for young men, or posing on one of the many fishing boats turned upside down on the beach.

Dad on Worthing beach (in 1956?)

Mum on the beach

Mum and Dad on their wedding day

Dad had served in the Second World War working as a sonar watcher on HMS *Fal*, in the seas surrounding Africa, watching for invading submarines which were trying to sail up the various rivers and channels.

Mum and Dad married in late August 1957 in Westcott, Surrey, and soon had 'number one son' Clive, followed by Alan and then John. I came along finally in 1970 after Mum and Dad had returned from

Australia. Dad had a collection of Coronation cups which he sold just to raise the money for the boat fare back to the UK, the journey taking eight weeks!

During my childhood days, Mum always flitted here and there, starting the day at 5 a.m, office cleaning, 'char' work for cleaning in private houses – you name it, she did it! Her role as Mum to me was always her first priority, hobbies and pastimes came last. With Dad so ill, Mum always made sure that I did not miss out on the usual birthday party and, aged 7, I can still remember the café/sweet shop that Mum built in the hallway of our house in Meadow Walk, Ewell, for all my friends to come along to. Mum made little purses for all the children, with real money inside, and we were able to go up and buy what we wanted to eat ... a brilliant idea and for once my party was the talk of the class!

Sadly, my memories of Dad are very vague, his ill health affecting us all in some way or another. I was not an easy child and as there was a six-year gap between me and my youngest brother, John, I grew up virtually as a single child. As a girl it was not the done thing in those days to go around with your brothers! Childhood memories are of Mum doing her endless washing days with the line always blowing with clothes and bedding, and so I got used to inventing my own playtime adventures in the 140-foot garden we had at the time.

Dad retired early from work as an accountant due to health issues with his chest (for many years during my childhood). Eventually, too much smoking over the years sadly resulted in lung cancer and his death in 1990. After this, Mum carried on regardless bringing in pennies here and there to support me until the glorified Child Benefit was introduced in the UK. Mum never remarried, something that in those days was frowned upon and she survived Dad by thirty years.

CHAPTER EIGHT

Where We Lived

Memories remembered as a child by Clive Walker ('number one son')

Iwas Mum's first child and was born in June 1958. When Mum introduced me to friends, she always said 'and this is Clive, number one son'. Not because I was favoured over my two brothers and sister but purely for accuracy reasons, I think!

Nana Beryl (left) with Mum and Ted Hayden, Beryl's second husband (right)
at the christening of Clive.

When I was a baby, we lived at 41 Park Way in Dorking. The house was a semi-detached from the 1930s or 1950s. I'm not sure how long we lived there exactly but we survived a house fire in August 1958. I slept in a small room at the front of the house overlooking the crescent of the road. I remember that we had a mangle for squeezing out water from washing; that was quite common at the time.

I remember walking to school (1962/63) and catching a bus on my own somewhere. It was a different era in those days; children travelled to school on their own and on buses and trains and not cars! My school was in Dorking at the bottom of the High Street. It's still there! I'm pretty sure this is now called Dorking Nursery School and Children's Centre.

Typically, I don't remember much else about the school apart from playing in the playground and the Beatles' song 'She Loves You (Yeah, Yeah, Yeah)', which was a big hit or number one at the time (1963).

Next, in the early 1960s, we moved to Chalk Pit Lane in Dorking (now renamed Yew Tree Road). It was a new house when we moved there; a semi-detached house in an unmade road (private road). I remember Mum and Dad's friends (in Ashcombe Road), Winnie and her husband. They had a son Timothy and daughter Lesley who were the same age or slightly older than me. We played and ran around in the large garden at the back of their house.

At the Chalk Pit Lane house, I cut my hand open whilst playing in the front garden. I don't remember this, or Mum and Dad taking me to hospital, but it was stitched, and I have the scar on my left hand.

Christmas at the house was an occasion when Mum and Dad and Uncle Ivan set up toys, such as a model farmyard or train set, in the dining room whilst we kids played in the front room. Then, there was a 'big' moment when they declared what they had done. Simple pleasures in those days!

We had a black car (an Austin 7, I think) with pop-up indicators and I remember trips in that. I can't recall everywhere we went but I remember being impressed that my dad could drive back home in the dark. One journey that I do remember was to Uncle Desmond's house (Mum's brother) in Warlingham, near Croydon, to visit him and his wife Betty and their children Paul and Nicola. We visited them regularly.

From the Chalk Pit Lane house, we used to walk from the end of the road through countryside and down to a farm during the hot summer months. This area is now Denbies Vineyard, Dorking.

Mum was always making her own summer dresses. She would cut a pattern out of paper and make the dress from material that she'd bought.

Dad worked at Cummins Hardware shop in Dorking as a bookkeeper. The shop is still there. Mum took me to visit his office once I remember.

Mum's mum, our Nana Beryl, died in 1965 when we lived in a house in Ashurst Road, Tadworth; we must have moved to the Tadworth house in 1964/65. I'm not sure why we moved but perhaps it was so that Beryl could live with us. It was an older house and Beryl lived in a room at the front. Sadly, I remember an ambulance taking Beryl to hospital and Mum saying that Beryl could see us waving as it drove away although we could not see into the ambulance because of its black windows. That was probably only a few weeks before she died.

The Tadworth house had a large rear garden where we cycled our bikes (me and my brother Alan).

Mum used to wake me in the mornings and light an old-style gas fire in my bedroom. The fire made a kind of whooshing sound when it ignited.

We walked to school in Tadworth; the school was down a long path from the road (although there was another entrance that we didn't use). I remember more about school in Tadworth compared with Dorking. However, my memories are mostly about playing in the playground and not much about the lessons!

I got into a fight walking home once and Mum had to take me to a dentist to fix a broken tooth.

CHAPTER NINE

Moving to Australia

By Clive Walker

A t about this time (1966/67), after Beryl died, Mum and Dad decided to emigrate to Australia. That must have been a massive decision. Dad's brother Bill Walker had lived in Melbourne when he was a young man and that may have inspired their decision. Also, Dad had a 'weak chest' (from a diphtheria illness as a child, not helped by his smoking) and they were motivated by a warmer climate that they thought would help. Although, as it turned out, the climate in Perth was too hot for them. Mum once said that they should have chosen Melbourne because it was more temperate.

Before the trip, we went to London to Australia House at least once, to complete the paperwork and get emigration visas. No Internet in those days!

Before leaving for Australia (travelling by boat), we sold the Tadworth house and lived in a flat in Sutton for a few days. This was the same time, November 1967, that the government devalued the pound. I remember this from a news report on TV.

With the decision made, my parents emigrated to Australia (under the Ten Pound Pom scheme) when I was 9 years old. We travelled to Perth, Western Australia, by ship in December 1967. The ship was the MV *Fairsea* which was owned by the Sitmar Line. On the voyage from Southampton, we stopped at Dakar and Cape Town, and eventually disembarked at Fremantle, near Perth.

It took about a month to get there! I remember boarding the ship, the places we stopped, climbing down lots of stairs to get to our cabin, watching the ship's wake as we cruised along, running round the upper decks, and playing lots of board games during the voyage.

Boarding the MV Fairsea: Clive, Dad, Mum, Alan (behind Mum), John (front)

Our family at the time was Mum, Dad, me, and my two brothers, Alan and John.

When we arrived, my dad had a job lined up, and we rented an apartment in Como, a suburb of Perth. I started at a new school and, unsurprisingly, I found it incredibly, um, Australian. For example, playing Aussie rules football on the sports field with my bare feet (ouch!) and having swimming lessons from the beach. That sounds nice now but it was a bit scary for me as a British boy, putting my head under the salty water and trying to avoid being stung by jellyfish!

After Como, my parents bought a new house (bungalow) in Lynwood, a bit further away from Perth, where there was a lot of new housing, much of which was bought by British immigrants like us.

We experienced an earthquake in Lynwood. I remember the house shaking and my mum and dad holding on to kitchen surfaces. I think this must have been the Meckering earthquake of 1968. Yikes!

Clive, John, Alan and Mum in Australia

Looking back, I think my dad probably had the best job of his working life when we were in Australia, Certainly, my parents never bought another new house. So, it was a shame in some ways when they decided that, after only a year in their new life, Australia was not for them.

I don't know all the reasons why they made that decision. They found the hot climate difficult, and I just think the lifestyle was too different to the UK. Also, my parents, especially my mum, wanted a daughter and perhaps they thought it was time to travel back before it was too late (my mum was 38 when my sister Lynette was born in the UK in 1970).

Whilst they were able to travel to Australia for £10 under the emigration scheme, for the return journey they had to pay the full fare and repay the outward journey as well. That must have been quite a sum. Dad had a collection of Coronation cups, mainly Royal Doulton ones, some of which he had to sell to pay for the journey home!

Dad, Clive, John and Alan in front of the SS Iberia

We travelled back to the UK, again by ship, on the SS *Iberia*. I remember waving from the ship to my parents' friends on the dock as we moved off. It was rather sad.

Another few weeks on the ship (more board games!) and we arrived back in the UK and moved into a rented house in Brockham, Surrey, and another school for me, before my parents bought their own house in Epsom. I was nearly 11 years old on our return.

Anyway, that's my 'Australia story'. Australia was an adventure and I've quite fond memories of it. A sunshine lifestyle is a great way to live when you are 9 or 10 years old.

CHAPTER TEN

Epsom and Ewell

By Clive Walker and Lynette Coates

After returning from Australia in 1969, we lived in a house in a pretty village called Brockham, in Surrey, for a few months. I went to school there for the summer term and remember being in class when the *Apollo 11* moon landing happened.

Over the summer, we moved to an older Victorian terraced house in Epsom, 24 Victoria Place and I started school at Longmead Secondary School in September 1969.

My sister Lynette was born in February 1970, and we moved to another house, 31 Green Lanes in West Ewell after that (1970 or 1971). It was a bigger house and was also close to my school but in the other direction. We lived there for a few years before moving in 1976 to 35 Meadow Walk, also in Ewell, a house very similar in size to Green Lanes but with a bigger garden.

The Walker Family at Meadow Walk in 1987

Looking back, my parents moved house a lot! Some of the family (Lynette!) have continued that 'tradition'.

Lynette continues the story with her memories

I was a child under the age of 5 when we lived at Green Lanes in Ewell. Mum was managing me, plus my three brothers through school, so life was rushed and hectic for Mum in her early forties. At this time, the UK celebrated the Queen's Jubilee with street parties and I can remember our neighbours having their party on the green with a very long table which ran down the middle of our road; I still have the commemorative coin all us children were given.

We moved to Meadow Walk, also in Ewell, when I was nearly 7. It was a bigger 1930s house with a long garden and with railway nearby; this was the year of the 1976 heatwave which went on for two months with ongoing droughts and water hosepipe bans.

By now, my brothers had left school and were either at college or university so life at home for Mum was less rushed but still as stressed due to Dad's ill health worsening by the month.

In those days we walked everywhere and were only 'privileged' to ride in our family car for special visits out on a Sunday.

Epsom was a nearby town to Ewell Village and had a leisure centre and swimming pool. Mum decided to learn to swim while I was learning at school and persevered with a lovely swim instructor called Jo who gave Mum the confidence to continue with it. In time she achieved various badges and even dressed up as a penguin and jumped into the pool raising money for charity; I still have Mum's swimming badges.

Mum tried many hobbies and joined many classes during the day, when I was in school, to develop her poetry skills and essay writing. She loved writing and her poems in this book show her wit and sincerity; she always loved to make the reader laugh which was usually me listening in awe, hoping one day I could write a poem or a story like that.

I wanted to join the Brownies by the time I reached the grand age of 8. Mum quickly got involved and became a Tawny Owl leader... she faced all the Brownie challenges alongside me and dressed up as a clown for the carnival parades that used to proceed through Epsom and Ewell.

During the 80s, as I turned 10 years old, Mum's marriage started to crumble due to Dad's declining health, so she got stuck into various cleaning jobs, leaving the house at 5am each morning and getting back before I went off to school. Mum also volunteered with the Invictus Disabled Club and helped at numerous jumble sales, always raising money for others even though she was keeping an eye on limited pennies in her purse. However, somehow, she always managed to fill up my pillowcase with Christmas presents along with an orange and chocolate money at the bottom.

Approaching my teen years, Mum was able to leave the house more and joined the local rambling group where she met her friend Doreen and they had many years of walking together. They also went on trips including visiting Paris and climbing the steps of the Eiffel Tower. Before moving house again, Mum also helped in a gift shop called Pollyanna in Ewell village and this was where she would write her letters of advice to me once I had left home; the letters are still treasured today.

I could easily fill up an A4 piece of paper and write down ALL the hobbies and pastimes that Mum tried and all the charities she was involved in over the years. Her time as a mum in the mid 70/80s era was the start that Mum needed as she reached her 50th year. As I turned 11, when we recorded ourselves on that old tape recorder, she was discovering herself ... Brenda, and her identity and purpose blossomed for the rest of her years, and she matured into the role of Nana to my children.

A mother is a role model and a job that Mum strived to complete to her best ability, she always tried, had a go, and most importantly faced every challenge with a smile and a laugh.

CHAPTER ELEVEN

Moving On

By Lynette Coates

Mum had many hobbies during my childhood; knitting and tapestries to name but a few, trying her hand at making dresses and blouses by following the 1970s clothing patterns, and card-making in later years. As a child growing up, I remember Mum was always in the kitchen baking something, scones, flapjack, fridge cake, quiches, home-made beef burgers or grits as she called them

Mum on a trip to Scotland

and her famous bubble and squeak. Mum liked to go on coach trips within the UK and I did join her for a few. I can remember when I took Mum to Italy, I think it was for her 70th birthday, she had never flown before and I shall never forget her face, full of excitement and awe as we took off in the plane!

Mum's favourite pastime, apart from reading, was writing poetry, mostly in the 1970s and 1980s during my childhood. She loved it and did have a knack of finding the right descriptive word and creating humour in some. She loved the well-known poet Pam Ayres and read many a poem by this lady.

As I mentioned at the beginning of this book, when I was 11 years old Mum and I recorded ourselves on a tape recorder. It was January 1981, it had snowed heavily overnight, and Mum thought it would be a laugh if we did a recital on her new tape recorder and send it to my aunts who lived in Scarborough. You can hear me playing on an old harp and recorder, singing the odd hymn or two and then, at the end of a 15-minute tape, Mum recites three of her most favourite poems, 'I Love You Mum', 'The Rocking Chair' and 'The Weather'.

After Mum died in 2020, I found that same tape, all those years later, that Mum had kept. Playing that back after forty years was a very special moment that I will always remember. It was priceless to hear Mum shouting out 'Hello Lynette' just as she used to do when she visited me or I called on her at home.

As I have grown up and have reached and passed my 50th year, I too love poetry and have written the odd poem or two since Mum has passed away. It has been a comfort for me, especially during the Covid pandemic the world encountered in 2020/21 and, as I write this, we are entering a third wave of this deadly disease. Mum kept all the poems she wrote and so I will share them with you all. Mum never managed to get any published in magazine or newspapers, she did try, so this is the next best thing that I can do for Mum in memory of her amazing talent in writing poetry.

The next section of this book contains all the poems that Mum wrote in the 1980s when we lived at Meadow Walk, where I grew up from the age of 6?, to when Mum finally sold up and moved into a house of her own, still in Ewell village. Dad (Reg) had died when I was 20 years old in the year 1990, sadly of cancer, aged 66. Mum moved to Spring Mews in Ewell and had her first home on her own for a few years; she loved this little house and owned the odd cat or two! Mum joined various groups and went on many a coach outing, joined lots of rambles in the countryside and even tried her hand at singing in a choir and made it up to the Royal Albert Hall singing in a group 'The Messiah'. Growing up during my teens, Mum and I would help at many a jumble stall and Mum made a lot of friends along the way. Always thinking of others before herself and having 'a purpose' in her life was something she always strived for, whatever her age and wherever she lived.

My leaving home, aged 16, was a massive blow for Mum but a decision she prompted me to make due to Dad's ill health at home. Mum in later years said it was like losing her left arm when I moved on with my life, up north initially. For a time as a mum she lost her purpose because all the brood had left the nest.

In the year 1997 the Walker family attended my wedding! Mum got involved with all the planning and the feeling of not being needed receded as she busily shopped for hats and wedding attire for herself. Our wedding gift from Mum was a hand-stitched embroidered sampler celebrating our wedding, which took Mum nearly a whole year to complete, a special gift which I still have today framed on the wall for all to see; a mother's devotion to her children is a special one. I was a proud daughter as I walked down the aisle to my future husband-to-be, knowing that Mum was standing in the front church pew without my dad, feeling as proud of my mum as she felt of me.

Mum and Lynette at Lynette's wedding

The Walker family at Lynette's wedding.
Left to right: John, Mum, Alan, Lynette and Clive.

Eventually, Mum made another big decision and moved down to Horsham where brother Clive and I lived and her duties of being a nana started!

Brenda with Clive in 2014

Mum lived at Lanyon Close in Horsham for nearly fifteen years and loved it. She made lots of friends via a Knit and Natter group and made her own cards for birthdays etc., often running a stall at the Cats Protection League's fetes. Mum spent her later years knitting baby T-shaped jumpers for orphans in Romania and she always kept busy and strove to have a 'purpose' to her life in the moment. Mum was a dedicated loving nana, she thrived in this new role and her words of wisdom have continued on with her grandchildren: Grace, Sam and Calum, who have their own special memories of eating their lunch in her summer house in the garden discussing the latest worry or problem.

The first poem is actually by me, written to Mum in the early hours after she had died, my own way of saying goodbye in the harsh circumstances the UK was in at the time with Covid raging its battle with the world. I wrote this poem at 3.30 in the morning, sitting in the hospital car park as the dawn was rising and the birds had just started to call the new day in. It's entitled 'Saying Goodbye'.

Poetry

Saying Goodbye

by Lynette Coates

At 3 a.m. this morning, within a night of stinging tears
Your beautiful, special life ended Mummy
Amongst a wave of fears
Oh my mummy, nana and best friend 'Goodbye,
I love you so.'
Saying those sorrowful words
Has been the hardest thing to do, I know
You were always by my side, through my child and adult days
Your love, devotion and pride shone out like rainbow rays
'I am Mother Hen,' you told me, 'I will always be there for you'
I am sorry Mummy, today I was not allowed to be, it's true!
Mummy died today from a virus
Which is killing our world's humanity
I was not allowed to be with you
Kiss and hold your warm loving hand
Life can be very cruel, ripping emotions apart and my sanity
Mummy, you are with your mummy now, and my daddy too
Stand proud, be Mother Hen in heaven I say
I salute you Mummy, my hero, now my angel above
There is no pain, you are at peace now, fly like a dove.
As I write this poem of words
Filled with heartache and priceless times
Time will heal my broken feelings
'Look Mummy, my poem rhymes!'
Time will help me to recover I will strive to be like you
Another Mother Hen, watch me Mummy do!

Xxxxxx Goodbye xxxxxx

Baby

A first born is the best by far
A sort of 'everlasting' star

It makes no difference who comes after
He filled your day with special laughter

To see him really there at last
Made all the efforts seem well past

His face, his tiny toes and feet
Your one concern 'Is he complete'

No other babe is quite the same
To bring you joy is why he came

A miracle rolled into one
Your long-awaited, new-born son.

BW

Written by Mum about the birth of Clive, 'number one son'.

All poetry comments by Lynette Coates

A Baby Girl

So now there is a daughter
A charming little girl

A sister for her brothers
Another one to spoil

They say that girls are made of
The sugar and spice
And boys are made of slugs and snails
Which isn't very nice

Well we don't care if it is the other way around
We have our dearest daughter
And she's the best that's to be found.

BW

Written by Mum after the birth of me!

What Makes a Parent Worry?

What makes a parent worry, create a scene, kick up a fuss
What is it that worries them and doesn't worry us?

If we stop up until midnight to watch the late-night movie show
Who cares that it will take all day for our shadowed eyes to go

And if we leave our clothes around, all strewn upon the floor
It will be days before they are noticed as Mum can't get through the
door

To make our beds each morning would really be a sin
You only need to pull them back in order to get in

It's 'Change your socks' and 'Clean your shoes'
And 'What time do you think this is?'
If we're one minute past the deadline then she's really in a tizz

We like to join our friends and copy exactly what they do
With punk hairstyles, slit skirts, pierced ears and these are just a few

Aw, Mum why won't you let me? I want to get them done
'Pierced ears are for the female sex and you've no right to, Son.'

'OK, you'll be a cyclist and that elusive pike you'll catch
But I've never seen a boxer wearing earrings win a match.'

I don't care if the school tie looks like a bit of rag around my neck
It goes all right with my new blue jeans and the shirt of yellow check

I hate the school meals service, I would rather have a bun
Two doughnuts and a milkshake are really much more fun
Who's heard of indigestion in one so very young
But I am feeling sort of sicky. 'Clean your teeth. Stick out your tongue.'

Worry, worry, worry, 'Have you done that? Will you do this?'
I always live in hope that perhaps one day these things will miss

I don't suppose I'd like it if they were never there at all
If Mum wasn't in when I got home to greet me in the hall

I guess I'd better mend my ways, it seems the only solution
Still I've got until the New Year before I make my resolutions.

BW

Not sure which of my brothers Mum was writing about!

A Letter to Auntie Floss

Dear Auntie Floss – A letter is much quicker said in rhyme
Though I know you'll think I've jobs with which to spend my time
But standing here, at the kitchen sink, with endless jobs to do
I thought 'Well why not try it, at least it's something new.'

So here I go with words a flow, though it might take all day
I'll try and write with all my might the words I have to say
Did you hear about the one I penned at work whilst wielding
broom?
'Twas about an order they'd received, and not a day too soon.

It seemed my request had been granted, to help me in my task
Of cleaning the office windows, I only had to ask
I have a lovely leather, a great big square of chamois
The task of cleaning windows now will really be quite jammy.

As I polish up the glass with it, the air will simply hum
Because it's smooth with a silky finish and soft as a baby's b—!
I've written several of these odes too numerous to mention
To raise a smile or hear a laugh is my only one intention.

They've been for passing driving tests and sick folk like yourself
And I only hope that if I'm sick – I'll get a few myself!
I went back to work on Monday after having three days off
I'd recovered from my heavy cold, I didn't have a cough.

They greeted me with smiles all round and asked me how I was
I felt like a real celebrity and not the one that 'does'
Their concern was really genuine and I didn't turn a hair
The fact the bins need emptying is neither here nor there.

When passing Sir upon the stairs, he said 'I'm glad you're back
As I am sure you are yourself' and he offered me a Hack
He said 'You know the visit that the VIPs are making
The cleaning you have done and the extra trouble you've been taking?
Well, they're not coming after all, it's all been changed by County Hall.'
I just replied 'What, no inspect?', and something else to that effect!

The 'fellers' in the workshop turned around and gave a cheer
They were pleased to see me and shouted 'Hello dear'
'That early morning sickness really stopped you getting here'
I said 'I only had the flu.' They chortled back 'That's something new.'

The fellers then, a group of six, said 'Here's just the job for you to fix,
so come on in, give us a hand, your help will really be quite grand.'
'We want to know if this wire's live, and incidentally, can you jive?'
I said 'It's overall inspection, you're looking dirty and not white
The laundry man is coming so, get 'em off!' They shouted 'RIGHT!'

We are still enjoying Keep Fit, we do it once a week
We pull the curtains tightly so that no one gets a peek at all our
exercises and hears our 'joyous' shrieks
Our hip rolls are enjoyed by all, but of this sort not edible
And the antics we get up to are really quite incredible.

Our ages range from teenagers to grannies young and old
And in our slacks and ballet tights we make a picture bold.
Give our love to all the nurses and not forgetting Doc
His name it seems has passed me by, (I don't think it's Dr Spock)

And thank them for all the care that they have given to
my Auntie Floss – and lots of love from all of us to you
Yours, Brenda

Written to my great-great aunt Floss when I was 7 years old.

The Innocence of a Daughter, Aged 7

When I am a lady I'll lie in bed all day
I won't have to work, but just have to play

I'll have my ears pierced and grow my hair long as can be
And anyone I ask can come to tea

I'll wear long silk dresses right down to my toes
There'll be ribbons all on them, all tied up in bows

I'll cook all the dinners, they'll be just what I
Like best most of all, lots of ice cream and pie

I don't think I shall have many babies at first
As they cry in the night 'cos they're dying of thirst

But perhaps I shall have just one and a husband may be
Oh, I can't wait for the day when I am a LADY.

BW

Did I say this to Mum aged 7?

Motherhood

It's just another phase we cry
As flopping in the chair we sigh
Exhausted at the end of day
Worn out by endless cries of 'Play?'
Oh for those babes in arms again
Those bundles of joy be it girl or boy.

Those sticky fingers, grubby knees
The endless 'I wants' but never 'Please'
The toiling up and down the stairs
Showing indifference to our cares
Defiance in his little face
Pretending not to know the place
And doesn't really care a jot
Whether he goes, or whether not.

Endless washing on the line
Living in hopes that it stays fine
Walks to the park, the ducks to feed
Eating the bread he doesn't need
The brotherly love and private wars
Between the sister he adores
The oft-tried patience of a mum-to-be
Who finds she's only a 'referee'.

'Who would be a mum?' is a question of old
But let me, to you, the secret unfold
It is the sweet **M**emories over the years
That are brought to mind, of the j**O**y and tears
The **T**rust that they give you, the **H**elp you give them
The **E**ternal love that nothing will stem
An unpaid servant some might say
But they're my **R**eward at the close of day.

BW

*A poem written in 1978 about my brother John and I, aged 14 and 8, the
word **M.O.T.H.E.R** spelt out in bold in the last verse.*

*Mum sent this poem off to two family magazines/newspapers in the hope
that they would publish the poem in time for Mother's Day. Sadly they
declined saying they did not have enough space or that the deadline had
passed. Mum kept their 'You have been unsuccessful' letters, still attached
to her typed-up poem; in those days you even sent them a stamped address
envelope for them to send back your poem, paid at your expense!*

Appreciation

I write this note with a lump in my throat, and really I must say
That when I read your rhyme with those words sublime it really
made my day

If someone does show a small mark of appreciation
It gives me a smile and makes it all worthwhile through all the
tribulations

Though I sometimes feel like a spinning wheel just going round and
round
It was with leaps and bounds, when your note I found

I worked with renewed vigour, and when I feel glum, as a
cleaner / mum, though my head might get a bit bigger
I have been told, though they're words of old, that hard work does
things to one's figure.

BW

Night-time Rituals

Come upstairs to kiss me before I go to sleep
Tuck me up more tightly so that from the sheets I'll peep
Leave a drink beside me as I might need one in the night
And don't forget I always want you to leave on the light.

What will you be doing when you go downstairs?
Do you have to leave before you have heard me say my prayers?
Here's my book from the library, it is one I haven't read
Would you see if there is a spider underneath my bed?

All right I'll be a good girl if you promise that you might
Just give me one more hug and kiss before we say 'Goodnight'.

xxxxx

Christmas decorations
Tinsel hung up high
Fairy doll upon the tree
Gifts with love for all to see.

(Just to finish.)

BW

My bedtime rituals as a child as I remember them, written into a poem by Mum.

Treasure

I am a 'treasure' undefined and help the sick, the old, the blind
It doesn't matter that my charge, is neither small nor very large
But it really is job satisfaction that gets me ready for some action
Each one has pride they wish to keep, and help's the last thing that
they seek
But once they know that I'm more a friend and have a hand or two to
lend
They greet me with a wave and smile which makes each day be more
worthwhile
And when my job with them is done, I realise it's been more fun
And hasn't always seemed to be like work in its capacity
There's a friendship there that doesn't stop when I've finished being
Mrs Mop!

BW

Mum always lent a hand to anyone in need.

Second-hand Shop

Yesterday's bargains now face rejection
Some showing signs of age and imperfection

Books that have been read once are placed in a pile
Inviting the reader to browse awhile

Higgledy-piggledy, such disarray
They could be yours for a few pence to pay

Everyone's cast-offs, some made-to-measure
Outfits worn once, merely for pleasure

Lampshades and china, teapots missing a spout
A gent's black umbrella, turned inside out

'What price?' and I offered, 'A snip did you say?'
'Yes, it's really the best of the bargains today.'

BW

*Mum never missed going to jumble sales, and bric-a-brac shops as her mum did –
and I do, too, to this day.*

Life's Like That

Why does it always start to rain when I am going out?

But when I'm home with all the chores
The sun delights those out of doors

And when I wait impatiently for the public transport bus
It seems that I could wait all day, they are all going the other way

And if I start to stand in line at the local P.O. counter
If I took a bet that the line I'd choose would be the quickest one …

I'D LOSE!

BW

Mum acting the fool!

Little Ship

Little ship inside a bottle, canvas pulled up tight
Do you ever wish that you could sail by stars at night?

Would you have chosen places full of mystery?
Instead of being just a ship of curiosity

Would your holds be full of timber, bales of cloth and spice?
Coffee, tea and sugar, and obviously rice

As each day we sailed with you, filling with elation
A never-ending journey in our imagination.

BW

Untitled

There once was a pussy, so sleek and so fair
Who possessed an ability (one really quite rare)
To balance a ball on the end of her nose
And yet still create quite an elegant pose
She could walk on a tightrope with such effortless ease
That she'd certainly cope with an unforeseen sneeze.

And oh such an agile young lady she'd be
That sometimes her feats would surprise even me
To swing on a bar at such incredible rate
Was surely I thought a temptation to fate.

Then one day it happened, I do not know how
(I wonder at times what she's doing now)
But along came a cat so handsome was he
That all she could do was to ask him to tea.

He said to her 'Surely you're not thinking of giving up all thoughts
of marriage to make this your living?'
What her reply was I just do not know, but I hear that they're
entering a foursome next show!

BW

Mum wrote this poem as one of her first ones in the early 1960s, but sadly never gave it a title ... during my childhood and into Mum's older years she owned numerous cats!

Weather

The weather's hot, the weather's cold
Why is the subject one of old?
We seek it here, we seek it there
It's spoken of most everywhere.

Here are two travellers on a train
Their mutual talking point is – RAIN
'How many inches fell last night?'
'That thunder gave me quite a fright.'

What would we do without the weather
To mention when we get together?
In cloakroom, bus and waiting room
Our faces turn to instant gloom.

'Oh! Not another day of sun'
'It's quite too hot to get things done'
In winter some just hibernate, until spring at any rate
And then we hear the constant shout
'DON'T CAST A CLOUT TILL MAY IS OUT.'

BW

The Rocking Chair

We went to a wedding on Sunday, there were 300 there
It brought back to me long-lost memories, and I also brought back a
chair

It is brown with a nylon stretch cover
That goes right across the seat
And with a detachable cushion, makes its comfort all complete

It was really meant for a jumble, or so I was told by Joy
But she knew I'd feel sorry for it
And I think she said this as a ploy

It was just that she'd had it a long time
And didn't like to see it go
To a house where it might get ill-treated
And would no respect for it show

So I accepted and was pleased about it
But then I forgot to say
That she didn't have to worry
It would 'live' for another day

And when I am feeling a bit weary
And not in the mood to roam
I shall sit with my own thoughts about me
And it will know it has found a good home!

BW

'I Love You Mum'

'I love you Mum', those words are dear
And they're printed on a souvenir
My daughter brought back home to me
The day she had been down by the sea

She came home, still dressed as a Guide
And turning from me tried to hide
The object clasped tight in her hand
She felt it wasn't all that grand

But I insisted that it was
As surely any mother does
'It's something that I <u>really</u> wanted'
(I didn't want her disappointed)

'I'll put it on a shelf up high'
Where I can see, as days go by
How much you really thought of me
The day you went down by the sea

I know it has not got much 'class'
That little tankard made of glass
But it's a gift that I'll always treasure
To prove a love beyond all measure.

BW

I still have this little glass tankard after all those years.

Drains

Drains are funny things you know
Always there but not on show
They like their solitude you see
Though they're not shy of you and me
DO NOT DISTURB is the order of the day
You can't divert their path in any way

Some are big and some are small
The worst are those not there at all
And if yours need a collection rota
It's best you provide an electric motor

You could of course erect a tent
Of privacy for good intent
Each spot you could then rediscover
Profuse with bloom, a mass of colour

The tag said 'Room for your own words'
But those have failed us now
To just say 'thanks' does not sound much
And we've thought with wrinkled brow
But really there's no more to say
We know you'll want no fuss
Except, just to remind you
You've not seen the last of us.

BW

The Terraces

The address had been given to me by the estate agent with apparent uninterest. I rather felt that he had given it to other prospective purchasers many times before and not received any commission in return. With the gas works in view as I turned the corner, I felt rather deflated myself at the prospect of buying property in this vicinity, but as soon as I saw the row of terraced cottages with their neatly kept front gardens and freshly painted exteriors, I was impressed with the look of homeliness that they had about them.

Each owner had obviously taken a pride over the years in maintaining both the property and the gardens, as although I had been told that they dated back to 1900 I rather felt that the modern-day properties would hardly look as well kept as these did 100 years later.

The gardens were a mass of colour, roses rambling over trelliswork in some, hollyhocks and delphiniums in another. Edges of lawns had been neatly trimmed, some curving and others in line with the hedge.

As I turned to open the gate of No. 35, I thought to myself that estate agent doesn't know what he has missed in not showing the clients around himself. That in itself would have been his 'commission' to have viewed such a pretty scene.

BW

A descriptive piece that Mum wrote for a literacy course, comments from the tutor were 'Good, convincing description'.

Yesterday's Treasures

Yesterday's treasures
Memories of old
Stories of history
The relics unfold

Year after year
As each decade has passed
Now all is exposed
For our eyes at last

What can we do now
To look to the future
When others will come after us.

BW

I Am An Office Cleaner

I am an office cleaner, my hours are nine till one
But if my work's done double-quick, by twelve I could be done

I rush around with mop and broom
And flick a duster round each room

I take a pride in all my floors
And shine the brass knobs on the doors

The desktops too, with loving care
Are polished up and should one dare

To slightly tilt their coffee cup
I get a sponge and mop it up

The telephones, too, get their share
'Cos hygiene is what's needed there

I sluice each mouthpiece with the lotion
And trust the germs will get the notion

In their heads to get outside
The smell you see they can't abide

My routine's ever-changing, and I never know what work
Is waiting there for me to do, and nothing do I shirk

Bins are emptied, stairs are swept, towels are laundered too
Nothing do I miss out, not even Sir's loo!

I come each day and gaze with awe
To see it rearranged once more

I have the right appliances, the tools to ensure speed
The up-to-date and modern aids, that every cleaner needs

The reconditioned polisher, so stalwart, big and brown
And as I'm going up the stairs, the Hoover that hangs down

I don't like it when it's raining
'Cos the mats don't dry their feet, but I don't go complaining
As my disposition's sweet

Excuse me while I fetch the mop, put on the smile so sunny
There goes that broom head, off again
Oh well, I need the money!

BW

Early Riser

No more working in the dark
Getting out of bed with the lark
Frozen fingers, frozen toes
With a drip upon my nose
Sweeping up and dusting round
Only me to make a sound
Empty office, silent 'keys'
Not a soul to hear my pleas
Armed with broom, dustpan and bucket
Full-up dustbin, (thinks ... I'll chuck it!)

There are no mats to sweep dust under
Through with wet feet they all blunder
In the workshop keep so busy
No use getting in a tizzy
Wash the floor yet once again
Pointless really, here's the rain
Feeling peckish, just for my sake
Wish I'd had the bowl of cornflakes
Here is something, dare I risk it?
No, they always count the biscuits.

BW

Memories of Mum's endless days as an early morning cleaner.

Personalities

I know that my second name's stupid
I've been told it often enough
My mum's second cousin was an idiot
And to take after him is sure rough
But as well as the sunburn and freckles
And the colour of her hair
I reckon I'm getting more like her
As folk tell me I'm not always 'there'
I know that my actions are varied
Because of this people get very vexed
It's not what I do at this minute
But rather what I might do next
I blame it on something that happened
At the moment of my birth
For my husband to get all the sympathy
While all I get is the mirth
But there sure is one good thing about it
I do make a lot of nice friends (I hope)
As I reckon that laughter is catching
So we all get alike in the end.

BW

Mum thinking about her anxious childhood fitting in.

Five Harassed Working Girls

Five harassed working girls going out one night
To see their friend at Bookham and join her in a bite.
Six harassed working girls glad to be alive
Met her at the doorway and picked up number five.

Six harassed working girls all raring to go
Asked one another 'What chocolate gateau?'
Six happy working girls thinking it all swell
Had salad, flans and cheesecakes – and stomach as well
Apricot gateau, one of Sylvia's – sublime
They had to keep on going to eat it all in time
Bubbly, coffee, brandy or gin, to leave just one crumb
Would be really a sin
By the end of round three the going was tough
And it wasn't just eggs that found themselves stuffed.

Five merry working girls were sorry to leave
Their sixth friend behind, but their journey they weaved
All speed had slackened at the end of the day
The last two were fretting 'Did they go takeaway?'
Twice left at the roundabout, take the next right turn …
'How long have you driven?' and 'Where did you learn?'
'Just follow that red Ford' … 'Look out for the bus'
'But they're nowhere in sight – oh, they're following us!'

The party's now over, our ways have to part
We wish it was now we were going to start
'Goodbye' … 'See you Monday' (if not before)
'Thanks for the lift right to my front door'
'What a nuisance it's snowing, still it might turn to rain'
'Wait, I've something to ask you: CAN WE DO IT AGAIN?'

BW

Working girl here has an innocent meaning.

Swimmer's Lament

I can't come out to play today, it really is a shame
But it's just the course of 'nature', that I've only got to blame
It is a flippin' nuisance because I've just regained my cool
And thinking that I might have taken a liking to the pool
The fact that Jo had mentioned her state of misery
Makes me think it might be catching
And I've come out in sympathy.

BW

The 'monthly curse' as it was called in those days.

Mum loved her swimming and would walk an hour and back from Ewell village to Epsom to enjoy her 30-minute swim.

For The Attention of Non-swimmers

Just listen while I tell you about my fervent wish
To 'Win the Pools' quite differently – and swim just like a fish
And so, while at the baths one day ('twas for a different reason)
I made a few enquiries at the start of the new season
I was informed quite cheerfully by someone we all call Jo
That she could get us swimming, and I thought 'I'll have a go'
Though with some doubts regarding my own capability
Because I didn't think she'd ever had one in before like me.

So feeling apprehensive I said I'd take the plunge
I looked as happy as a lark, but felt limp as any sponge
I made sure the orange armbands were blown up like a balloon
And thought the next half-hour for me cannot go too soon
'Now were your feet then off the bottom?', 'Keep your shoulders and chin down,'
But when I went 'down under' it wasn't kangaroos I found
They told me there were goldfish on the bottom of the pool
But when I looked the second time, I really felt a fool.

I greeted them with sickly grin, and tried to see the joke
My thoughts were in turmoil. But I just said 'Hello folks,'
They said 'You've come along to try again, you'll do it never fear,'
I said 'I'm just scared rigid, and to prove it I am here!'

'Now take it easy, just go slow, and put your trust in me,'
I thought – you mad and reckless fool – and slowly counted three.
'Now just get past that second lane, don't simply hang about,'
'That's sooner said than done,' I gasped because my innards say 'Get out.'

I've lost near half a stone in weight, my nerves are in a tizz
I'm feeling like a lemon before it gets the fizz
I suppose I'd better humour them, keep going for a bit
Or is the reason simply that I am liking it!

'Keep those arms a moving, one-two,' Joan Forbes doth cry
If I can just keep going, I might get there by and by
'Don't let those legs forget to move,' says Jo with added smile
'I've taught some strokes while I've been here
But I've never seen that style.'

'You're doing well considering, as lessons you've not had many,'
'Yes, thanks a lot, but now I've got to go and spend a penny!'
I think I might be getting it, my confidence renewed,
My breaststroke's getting stronger and Jo says I have improved
I've just swum in from three lanes out with airless armbands on
I cannot swim without them because I like to keep them on
The fact they're at my elbows shows they're really just a con.

My tenth lesson's up on Friday but I guess they'll let me stay
I'm hoping that this odd ode might simply make their day
Armbands are going to have to go but to say goodbye would be a
shame,
So I'm going to keep on coming because I'm ever so glad I came.

BW

Mum raised a lot of money for charities over the years in sponsored swims and even jumped in dressed as a penguin!

What? No Swimming!

We regret that our Xmas newsletter is short
But we have both been busy, we'd not given it thought
And now that the festive season is here
Our brains are so addled with water we fear
We shall not be able to be any good
At dishing up turkey, Xmas crackers and pud.

We've tried all the Baths – Morden, Banstead and Cheam
We even tread water whilst still in a dream
It's either too costly, too warm or too cold
So you think it will help us grow gracefully old?
Our language at times … well we cannot repeat
And even some floors are too hard for our feet.

We are missing the 'comforts' of Epsom you see
Like having a door on the place where we —-!
We are both quite determined, we'll never give in
And have made up our minds to just bear it and grin.

At Morden the pool is so deep and too long
At Banstead the water is definitely strong
We reckon that Cheam is perhaps the best place
But only till April if we can still stand the pace
We wonder at times of what progress we've made
We are feeling just like two black sheep that have strayed.

Our housework is suffering, there's dust on the shelf
If they want any cake, we say 'Make it yourself!'
They don't know what's hit them … really shook to the core
We don't care and wish that we'd done it before
And besides that we've got some more lined up for you
There's Olive and Leila, Patricia and Sue
And the son of our family doctor too.

We are right in the dog house and alas and alack
We guess that our present this year is the sack
But we are not going to worry, we are not going to fret
We know who our friends are …
That's THE DOG AND LYNETTE!

BW

When swimming pools were closed for refurb!

Rambling

R Remember those walks through rain, snow and sun
A And counting the stiles one by one
M Mud up to our ankles, a fall 'A over T'
B Beware of the bull signs, or is it a she?
L Lingering over lunch with our now absent friends
I Including the ducks for our scrap ends
N No doubt about it there will always be
G Good memories of a friendship between you and me.

BW

Written by Mum when her close friend Doreen moved back to New Zealand.

Mum and Doreen in Paris in 2001

Removal Day

Removal day is on us, the van is just outside
It's big and brown with flap dropped down
And everything's inside
I don't know why it is, but on occasions such as these
The house seems more a friend, a fact I cannot comprehend
It seems however much I try, I don't want to say 'Goodbye'.

As I look around intent to find, anything we've left behind
My searching gaze instead is caught
By signs our occupation's wrought
The paint spilt on the lino floor, doggy scratches on the door
The loose catch on a cupboard, the larder door that stuck
The slightly tilting front gate, where the kids have run amok.

There is something here I thought, that we cannot take away
It's part of all of us – our living day by day
Aims, ambitions, joys and fears
That we have felt throughout the years
The door's now closed on all of that, the future is ahead
Goodbye old friend, we're going to fill
Another house instead.

BW

Mum moved house a few times. Reading this poem back, it might have been written when she moved from Meadow Walk in Ewell, which was my family home.

To Cherish – As Time Goes By

As one has said to their Old Dutch
It hasn't seemed a day too much
Our years have grown to twenty-five
And still we've kept our love alive
We've watched our one and only son
And gloried in all that he's done

We've had our joys and troubles
Our laughter and our tears
But wouldn't want to change a thing
In any of those years
For each and every incident
Has brought us where we are
And when we've wanted comfort
Have not had to look very far

Our love has just been strengthened
By the passing of each day
Although at times we haven't known
Exactly what to say
Each one's love is different
Expressed by just a sign
It only needed one small glance
To know that you were mine

'For every man there's a woman'
We hear the singer cry
We're glad we have each other still
To cherish – as time goes by.

BW

Autumn

Green leaves of autumn turning to gold
Spiralling down to the ground, turning cold

Evenings are darkening, winter is nigh
Birds are aloft in migratory sky

Apples are strewn in the grass 'neath the trees
Blackbird is taking his breakfast with ease

Hear the dawn chorus through fast falling rain
Imploring those on their way, 'Come back again'.

BW

God's Love

The daffodil arrives in spring
The sight of one will make you sing
The tulip standing tall and proud
Is only happy in a crowd ...
I am a pimpernel so shy
And hide my face as you go by

I like the sun to help me show
How much I grow and grow and grow
A rose might ramble out of hand
But even so the sight is grand
In spring the blossom on the trees
Is turned to honey by the bees

The wind is the carrier of our seeds
We are dandelions and only weeds
We make a pretty picture each
Some tall, some short, some out of reach
But God loves us all without a fuss
(We are all different, each one of us)
And so we ought to do our best
To help those less fortunate from the rest.

(And I wasn't just thinking about Nature.)

BW

Cure For The Blues

Here's a few rules we all must follow
Though like a pill they're hard to swallow

Take a look at what's outside
For those not blind don't need a guide
Imagine if we couldn't see
How dreadfully dull it all would be
And if each day we couldn't hear
The words from those we hold most dear
To speak to each we love the best
And take away those said in jest

To give a sympathetic ear to other people's woes
'Cos each one of us has problems, that's the way life goes
And though at times for you to see, tomorrow is another day
For you to conquer in your way

Just count your blessings one by one
And after this when you have done
Stop to take a look inside
Some love lies hidden and needs a guide
It's hard to realise you see
That all this love of ours is free.

BW

I Wish I Was There Again

I wish, how I wish I was there again
In such lovely surroundings, (apart from the rain)
To think we had two weeks – just us and the kids
To negotiate all of those bends, and the skids!

Oh, I wish I was there again
The little thatched cottage just down the lane
The quaint-looking Rayburn that stood in the gloom
And all the mod cons – mop – bucket and broom!

Oh, I wish I was there again
That big double bed with checked counterpane
The nightly excursions with child under four
To the outside loo with the latchless door.

Oh, I wish I was there again
Playing Scrabble and Ludo – with still endless rain
The cockerel's first call waking us from our sleep
The mooing of cows and the baaing of sheep.

Do I wish I was there again?
I would swap those vacations to exotic places
For just one more week with those innocent faces
And recapture my youth down memory lane

Yes, I wish I was there again.

BW

A Year Has Passed

by Lynette Coates

A year has passed now, an emotional one I have had
I have cried and smiled at the memories
Even though some have been bittersweet and sad

COVID lockdowns have enveloped my time of mourning and grief
Spring has launched around me
Carrying a sense of reassurance and relief

Today the birds are singing as loud as they did last year
On the day we laid you to rest Mum, my face wet with a tear

Time is all that is needed I was told
Grief can take a while to surface and unfold
It's a hard challenge in life to face
To rise again with confidence and to feel bold

I look forward to having the family hug
That I could not have last year on that sad day
To see people's faces again smiling
Normality is the answer I say

The cuckoo has just called in the distance
Awaiting its eager reply
Carry on flying with the birds Mum
I will follow your mummy advice and 'Just try'.

Lynette Coates – 6 May 2021

A New Year Dawns

by Lynette Coates

In the twilight hours of dawn and dusk owls start their hoot
Waiting in hope to hear a reply
Blackbirds announce the dawn rise with a flute-like sound
Finishing in unison as they fly
A robin waits with anticipation on a gatepost
For the odd crumb of bread
Little Jenny Wren finds shelter under hedges
Flitting back and forth foraging for grubs ahead
Frozen bird baths and ponds with life resting dormant underneath
Winter bulbs surge upwards towards the light
A hint of green colour shows upon the heath
Clusters of snowdrops gather with drooping heads
Bowing in in unison with dignity
Daffodils displaying their bright yellow coats
Sheltered against a majestic ancient oak tree
Early morning fog gives the lake an ethereal appearance
The north wind blows in snow
Rain brings forth a rainbow through captivating clouds
Leaving a glistening rose hip and sloe
Cold rosy cheeks on human faces

A bracing wind whips through scarves wrapped around
Sheep huddle as one in the bucolic landscape
Camouflaged in the crisp frosty surround
Winter recedes with spring approaching
The hollow knocking of the woodpecker is heard
The shortest day is behind us
Daylight lengthens minute by minute
Skittish squirrels chirred
As one year finishes a new year will always dawn
Bringing hope, courage and determination
Nature will always continue to nurture and grow around us
In our world's creation.

Written after a pandemic year filled with much loss of human life

Lynette Coates – 2021.

Final Words

By Lynette Coates

And so, our lives continue, families grow, and the next generation starts on their own exciting lives ahead. Mum was lucky to see each grandchild reach 21, she even saw me reach 50 and had a slice of birthday cake a few weeks before she died in hospital. Mum was diagnosed with dementia in the last few years of her life, which worsened considerably, she also had a terminal diagnosis of bowel cancer in her final year. For Mum the frustration of not knowing in her mind what was real or made up was hard to accept but, in a way, the dementia thankfully helped Mum to forget that she had cancer and, gracefully, Mum kept her dignity and never once forgot who we were and always remembered my dad.

I shall never forget my last visit to Mum before the hospital went into lockdown, not knowing when I would see Mum again or *if* I would see her again. We had always in our lives waved to each other as we said 'Cheerio' if I was ever taking the train somewhere or the bus Mum would be there waving like a maniac, but on this occasion I said, 'Until we meet again, Mum,' and then I did my silliest wave ever, like she used to do! A priceless memory of Mum looking up to the sky, laughing her head off and waving as if she was the Queen. I will hold that special moment in my heart forever, my precious mummy, my queen.

Due to the ongoing pandemic of Covid the world is still enduring we never have had a memorial for Mum to celebrate her life. Finding Mum's childhood memoirs and publishing this book for Mum is our way of remembering a special lady and her achievements; she will never be forgotten.

I shall finish this book with Mum's final words to her family and friends written many years ago on that old, battered Corona typewriter.

Laugh and grow fat as my mum would say, you will not be without me – ever – I live on within each of you, and what a joy it has been. Each day as you say or do something you will think, 'Mum used to say or do that', so you will each be living on in my memory and your children in yours ... and so it will continue.

Love you all .... Mum, Brenda, Nana xxxxx

Brenda's memoirs were dedicated to her grandchildren, Grace, Sam and Calum.

Brenda with Grace in 2019

Brenda with Sam

Brenda with Calum in 2019